Food to Eat

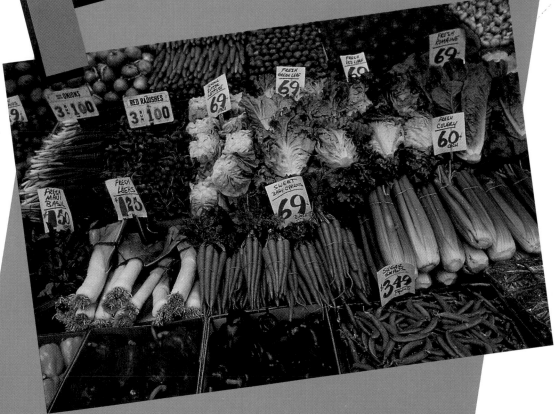

by Catherine Peters

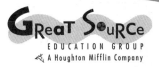

GReaT SOuRCe
EDUCATION GROUP
A Houghton Mifflin Company

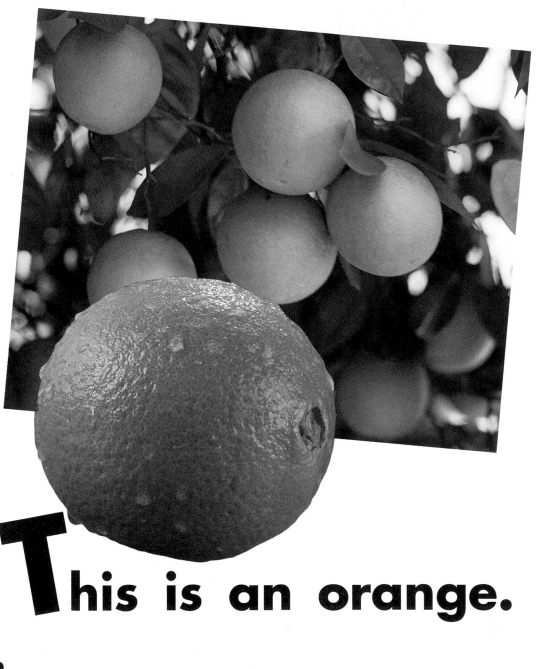

This is an orange.

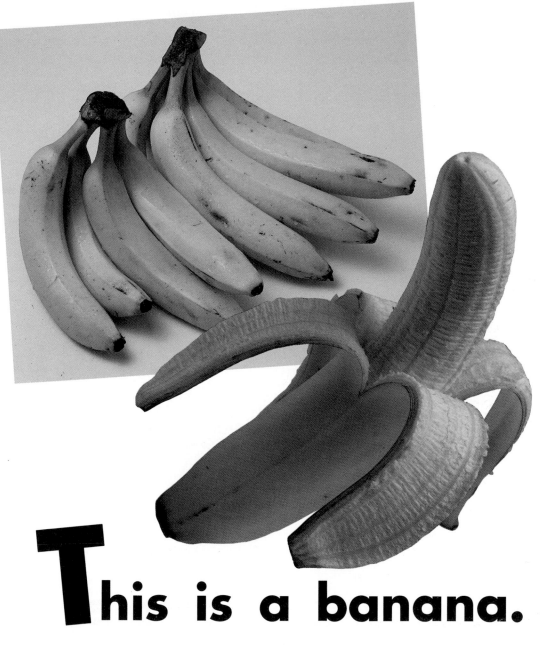

This is a banana.

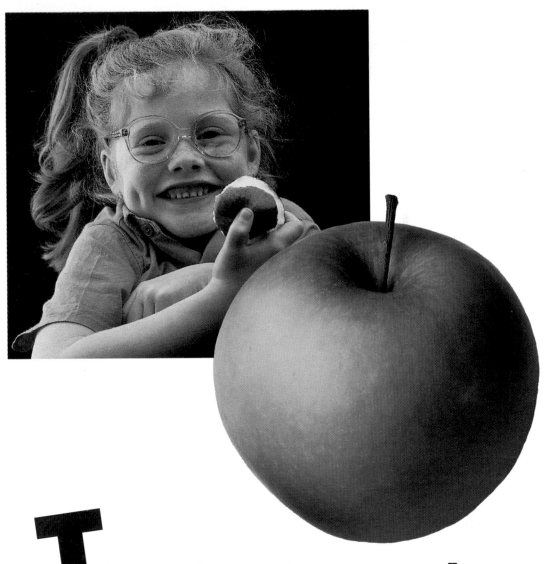

This is an apple.

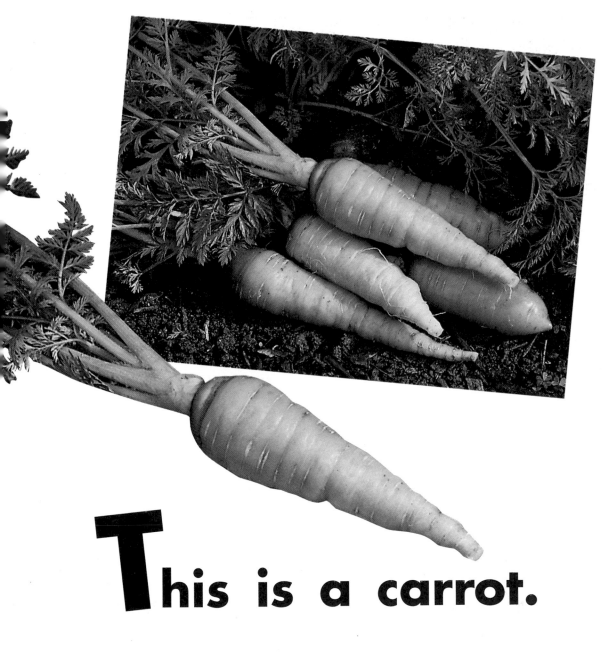

This is a carrot.

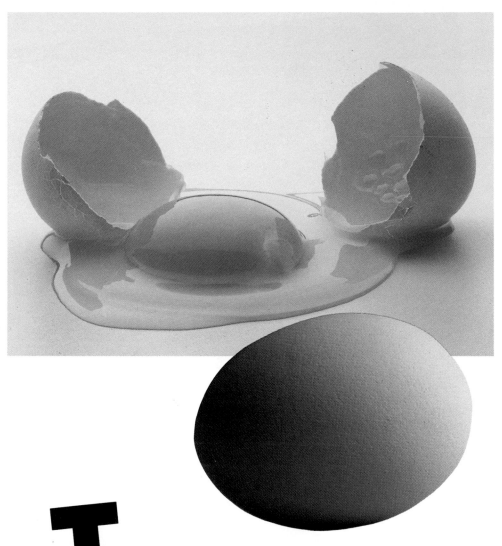

This is an egg.

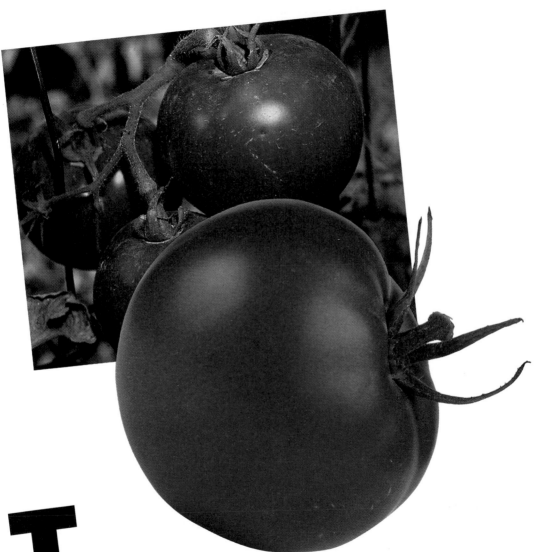

This is a tomato.

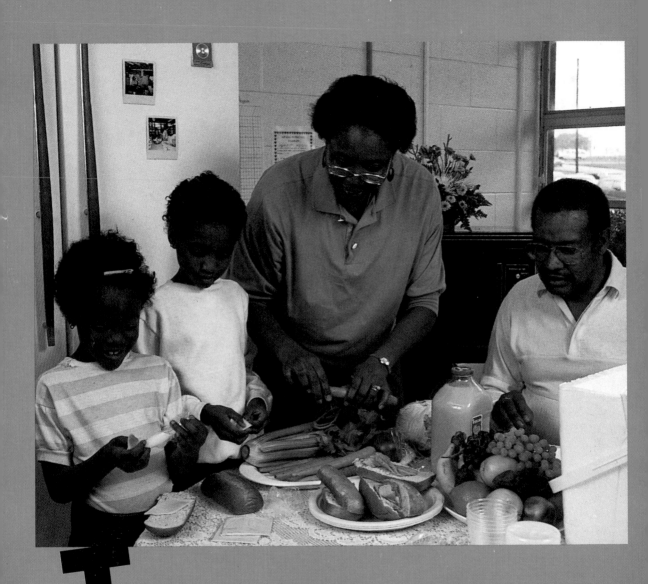

This is food to eat.